K HALID SHEIKH 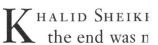 the end was n wing lawyers who'd volunteered their services to the al Qaeda Defense Bar had pulled out all the stops in their eight-year jihad against Bush-style counterterrorism. Their *bête noire* had been the military commission system, the time-honored procedure for trying war crimes. President Bush had attempted to reinstate it after the massacre of September 11, 2001. The effort reflected America's determination that Islamic terrorists were not everyday criminal defendants to be swaddled in the Bill of Rights, but military enemies to be captured, imprisoned and executed.

For a while, the lawyers had derailed the effort, flooding the federal courts with challenges to the commissions' legitimacy. But the tide had turned. Judges had finally declined further obstructions. Commission trials had begun, and two al Qaeda operatives were quickly convicted. When KSM had been grabbed in Pakistan back in 2003, he smugly told his captors that he'd talk to them in New

York ... with his lawyer. To his chagrin, though, the maestro of 9/11 soon learned that the lawfare party of the 90s was over. He found himself talking to the CIA. And now it was December 2008. Stuck in Guantanamo Bay and facing the imminent prospect of a military trial, KSM made an announcement: he and four fellow 9/11 plotters were prepared to plead guilty – to brag that they were guilty – and to proceed to execution and Allah's great orgy in the sky.

Meanwhile, in Washington, a tectonic shift was under way. Barack Obama was blowing into town, fueled by a radical base that saw Bush, not KSM, as the real war criminal. Obama's campaign spokesman Eric Holder had fed the frenzy, promising the base a "reckoning": An Obama administration would hold Bush officials accountable for what he portrayed as serial transgressions against the Constitution and international humanitarian law. When that Obama administration became a reality, Holder was tapped to be its attorney general. He threaded his new Justice Department –

particularly its upper tier – with veterans of the al Qaeda Bar. The reckoning was at hand.

With a lot of palaver about ending Bush's "politicization" of justice, Holder went banana republic, turning his vast prosecutorial powers against the Obama Left's Most Wanted list. Investigations were pursued against Bush administration lawyers and CIA interrogators. Holder made commitments to assist foreign tribunals considering "torture" charges. He shoveled into the public domain previously classified information about CIA interrogations and other Bush counterterrorism initiatives. And finally, in November 2009, after pulling the plug on KSM's military commission – in a case that was on the verge of wrapping up – the attorney general made the stunning announcement that the 9/11 jihadists would be transferred to Manhattan for prosecution in the civilian justice system. Holder gave KSM his wish: a New York City stage where, after rifling through government intelligence files for the next two years, he gets to put the United States on trial for the stratagems that protected Americans from reprises of 9/11. It is the ultimate politicization of justice by a master of the game.

Holder gave KSM his wish: a New York City stage where he gets to put the United States on trial for the stratagems that protected Americans from reprises of 9/11. It is the ultimate politicization of justice by a master of the game.

REAL POLITICIZATION OF JUSTICE

During the tenure of Attorney General Alberto Gonzales, Democrats caterwauled about "politicization" at the Bush Justice Department. The hyperbolic allegation was largely based on Bush's firing of eight U.S. attorneys so they could be replaced by new appointees favored by influential Republicans. That sounds nefarious, but it is done by every administration. United States attorneys are executive branch officials who serve at the pleasure of the president and can be removed by the president for any reason – or no reason. The 93 U.S. attorney slots are coveted patronage, infused by political intrigue as senators and governors jockey to influence appointments in their states. Indeed, at the start of his first term, President Clinton summarily fired all but one of the incumbents. Charging that justice is "politicized" because of the replacement of U.S. attorneys, an inherently political exercise, is no more sensible than claiming that the air we breathe is polluted by carbon dioxide. (Yes, yes, I know.) Still, the charge gained traction in Democrats' media-fueled campaign against the hapless Gonzales, a Bush confidant and thus a useful proxy for deriding post-9/11 national security policies.

The mantra that the Bush Justice Department had been "politicized" could not conceal the gaping hole in the Left's indictment. There was no evidence of the only politicization that actually matters: the basing of *enforcement decisions in individual cases* on politics. A president's choice of lawyers and enforcement priorities is political by nature, and we wouldn't want it any other way in a democracy. But Americans have always drawn a bright line between staffing and enforcement. When it gets down to the brass tacks of real investigations, politics has no place.

DOJ's prosecution of individual legal cases must reflect our constitutional commitment to equal protection under the law. That is, it must not be corrupted by political considerations. The rule of law, part of the glue that holds a free society together, is dependent on evenhanded, nonpolitical law enforcement. That is why trial judges routinely instruct juries that cases must be decided strictly on the evidence, "without fear or favor." Furthermore, freedom itself hinges on robust political debate, a fundamental constitutional value. Law enforcement that targets political adversaries, criminalizes policy disputes and shields political cronies is an aspect of tyranny.

When we talk about the bedrock principle that justice must not be politicized, it is this administration of justice that we mean. Yet it

---

Law enforcement that targets political adversaries, criminalizes policy disputes and shields political cronies is an aspect of tyranny.

---

is precisely the administration of justice that has been hijacked by partisan politics in the Obama administration.

PAST IS PROLOGUE

Obama knew exactly what he was getting with Eric Holder. Holder had been Justice's number two official for the last three years of the Clinton administration. He became the most influential actor in the most unabashedly politicized Justice Department in American history. He was the prime mover behind the infamous pardon of Marc Rich, one of the FBI's "most-wanted" fugitives. Rich had been sought since the 1980s for millions in fraud, tax evasion and trading with America's enemies. In 1999, while Rich continued to evade capture – flitting across the globe to avoid prosecution, which is itself a crime – Holder flouted Justice Department protocols against negotiating with the agents of a fugitive. He advised Rich's chief attorney, former Clinton White House Counsel Jack Quinn, on how to deal with federal prosecutors in New York in his effort to get the case dismissed. When that didn't work, Holder steered Quinn into position to lobby Clinton directly for a pardon – circumventing the rigorous Justice Department pardon process, which the deputy attorney general oversees. Holder kept New York prosecutors in the dark about the pardon application, ensuring that President Clinton heard only Quinn's specious claims. He then pushed the pardon over the goal line by recommending that it be granted during the frantic final hours of the Clinton administration.

The shocking Clinton pardons were politics at its crassest. An inveterate careerist, Holder extended his helping hand in hopes that Quinn, a top confidant of Vice President Al Gore, would look favorably on his quest to become attorney general in a Gore administration. Holder had been tending carefully to that project since his arrival at DOJ in 1997, when he used his influence to block the appointment of a special prosecutor to probe Gore's black-and-white felony violation of campaign finance laws. Holder also politicized the pardons process in 1999 for the benefit of Hillary Clinton's 2000 Senate campaign – acceding to his president's desire to pardon *terrorists*, specifically, Puerto Rican separatists, including members of the FALN, a group responsible for more than 130 bombings in the United States.

The Clinton-era Holder sang the same paeans to "transparency" as the new-but-not-so-improved model. Back then, as now, he also dutifully stonewalled Congress – successfully claiming executive privilege to thwart attempts to get to the bottom of the FALN pardons. He was not as fortunate, though, in the Rich affair. A congressional committee aptly described Holder's conduct as "unconscionable"; inferred that Quinn's "key position to assist Holder's chances of becoming Attorney General" had been "a powerful motivation for Holder"; and implied that Holder had not been forthright in testifying that he had failed to inform himself about the nature and extent of Rich's criminality. That last condemnation would no doubt have been even stronger had the committee realized that in 1995, when he was the U.S. attorney for Washington, D.C., *Holder had actually targeted Rich* – going so far as issuing a press release to trumpet his office's successful suit against a Rich company (during the settlement of which Holder's subordinates had obtained an affidavit directly from Rich, the fugitive).

Although out of power in the Bush years, Holder had not run out of political chutzpah. When the country erupted in anger after 9/11, Democrats who'd failed to address al Qaeda's provocations during the 90s knew they needed to project antiterrorist resolve. Holder rushed to the fore. In 2002, he admonished CNN that "we are in the middle of a war," and thus, captured terrorists should be detained without trial as "combatants." He explained that under governing "precedent," we could "detain these people until the war is over." And Holder was emphatic in rejecting the claim that al Qaeda had Geneva Convention rights: "One of the things we clearly want to do . . . is to have an ability to interrogate [terrorists] and find out what their future plans might be, where other cells are located." Terrorists, he elaborated, "are not, in fact, people entitled to the protection of the Geneva Convention." But what about America's reputation in the world? Wasn't Holder worried about upsetting the Europeans? "Those in Europe and other places who are concerned about the treatment of al Qaeda members," he scoffed, "should come to Camp X-ray [at Gitmo] and see how the people are, in fact, being treated."

Time went by, the Left evolved, and, true to form, Holder evolved along with it. Covington & Burling, the Washington law firm at which the former deputy attorney general was a senior partner, threw in its lot with the al Qaeda Defense Bar, seeking the release of the very prisoners Holder had earlier called for detaining. Simultaneously, the Obama campaign – viscerally antiwar and committed to the law-enforcement approach to counterterrorism – caught fire. Sensing another chance to become attorney general, Holder signed on as a top adviser and spokesman.

That meant serving up red meat to the base, and the adaptable Holder rose to the occasion. In a June 2008 stem-winder at the Left-leaning American Constitution Society, he inveighed against Guantanamo Bay, calling it "an international embarrassment." It had to be closed because "a great nation should not detain people, military or civilian, in dark places beyond the reach of law." The amnesia-stricken Holder was now theatrically horrified by Bush counterterrorism: Never had he believed he'd see a day when the "Supreme Court would have to order the President of the United States to treat detainees in accordance with the Geneva Convention." Nor was his revulsion confined to Gitmo. Bush officials, he summarized, had "authorized the use of torture, approved of secret electronic surveillance against American citizens, secretly detained American citizens without due process of law, denied the writ of habeas corpus to hundreds of accused enemy combatants, and authorized the use of procedures that violate both international law and the United States Constitution." Due to Bush's "needlessly abusive and unlawful" policies, Holder bleated that we had "lost our way with regard to [our] commitment to the Constitution and to the rule of law." As a result, we'd "diminished our standing in the world community" and rendered ourselves "less, rather than more, safe." It would not be enough for an Obama administration merely to reverse these policies. Holder titillated the crowd with a promise: "We owe the American people a reckoning."

WHICH SIDE ARE WE ON?

The first thing one notices about the Justice Department's transition from Bush to Obama is the challenge involved in getting the highest-ranking lawyers engaged in the most significant cases. During the Bush years, national security was inarguably the nation's top priority and Justice Department lawyers were fully engaged in the war on terrorism. By contrast, key Obama administration lawyers spent those years at law firms and institutions that enthusiastically provided *pro bono* legal representation and issue advocacy for America's enemies. (Yes, American lawyers consider the representation of al Qaeda operatives who target the American public to be the noble work they provide free of charge under the haughty label *pro bono publico* – "for the public good.")

Under the profession's conflict-of-interest rules, this has rendered the Obama administration lawyers ineligible to work on cases in which their former firms participated. That includes Attorney General Holder, whose firm

---

Holder's firm, Covington & Burling, made representation of the terrorists detained at Guantanamo Bay its most lavishly resourced no-fee project, 3,022 hours in 2007 alone.

---

made the terrorists detained at Guantanamo Bay its most lavishly resourced no-fee project (3,022 hours in 2007 alone). Covington & Burling's Web site proudly boasts about the firm's success in urging federal judges to grant its "clients" – 18 enemy combatants – new "rights under the Fifth Amendment and the Geneva Conventions." Also touted is the firm's key role in the 2006 *Hamdan v. Rumsfeld* case, in which the Supreme Court invalidated the Bush military commissions. The lead counsel for Salim Hamdan – Osama bin Laden's personal driver and bodyguard – was Neal Katyal, a former Georgetown law professor who is now the Justice Department's deputy solicitor general. Holder's Deputy Attorney General David Ogden – whose clients included child-pornography producers and pro-abortion extremists – worked at a firm that represented three enemy combatants and that figured prominently in *Boumediene v. Bush* (2008), in which the Supreme Court granted the alien detainees a U.S. constitutional right to challenge their detention in civilian federal court. The problems go well beyond Holder, Ogden and their top staffers (drafted from these same firms). Similar conflicts plague, among others, Associate Attorney General Thomas Perrelli (DOJ's No. 3 official) and the chiefs of both the Criminal and Civil Divisions, Lenny

Breuer and Tony West (the latter volunteered his services to represent John Walker Lindh, the so-called "American Taliban," a U.S. national now serving a 20-year sentence after making war against his country).

It bears observing that the leadership Obama and Holder envision for Justice is not yet fully in place. The Senate has blocked the nomination of an academic, Dawn Johnsen, to lead DOJ's Office of Legal Counsel. OLC is the lawyers' lawyer, driving administration legal policy by authoritatively interpreting the law for the attorney general. Its credibility is derived from its reputation for apolitical, academic discipline – informing policymakers of what the law is, rather than what staffers would like it to be. Despite the Democrats' filibuster-proof majority, Johnsen has been stalled because she is an unabashed political ideologue. Besides the obligatory tropes about Bush war crimes, she sees the law as a tool for enacting "the progressive agenda": "universal health care, public funding for childcare, paid family leave, and . . . the full range of economic justice issues, from the minimum wage to taxation policy to financial support for struggling families." The main impediment to her nomination, however, is her bizarre claim that abortion restrictions (e.g., the denial of public funding) are analogous to violations of the Thirteenth Amendment's proscription against slavery – an argument she posited in a Supreme Court brief while serving as the legal director of the National Abortion Rights Action League. According to Johnsen, a pregnant woman "is constantly aware for nine months that her body is not her own: the state has conscripted her body for its own ends." The justices were unmoved, as they were by her equally startling theory that, absent government-provided abortion counseling, many women would be left without "proper information about contraception" – leaving them "losers in the contraceptive lottery [who] no more 'consent' to pregnancy than pedestrians 'consent' to being struck by drunk drivers."

Holder has a freer hand with posts that do not require Senate consent. That explains his hiring of Jennifer Daskal, a lawyer with no prosecutorial experience, to work in Justice's National Security Division. Her qualification? Daskal is a left-wing activist who advocated on behalf of al Qaeda prisoners while serving as the "counterterrorism counsel" (yes, *counter-*terrorism) at Human Rights Watch. She has, for example, claimed that KSM may not be guilty of the unspeakable acts he can't stop bragging about because, after all, Bush may have tortured him into confessing. She lamented that another detainee, "a self-styled poet," suffered abuse in U.S. custody when he "found it was nearly impossible to write poetry anymore because the prison guards would only allow him to keep a pen or pencil in his cell for short periods of time." And she has been a staunch supporter of the terrorist detainee Omar Khadr, who was 15 when he allegedly launched the grenade that killed U.S. Army Sergeant First Class Christopher Speer. Daskal frets that a prosecution would violate Khadr's "rights as a child." Khadr recently turned 23.

Holder has assigned Daskal to help shape

detainee policy.

With this cast of characters at the wheel, the Justice Department is pursuing three "national security" priorities: (a) repudiating Bush-era counterterrorism policies while reinstating the pre-9/11 law-enforcement model; (b) increasing the rights of terrorists; and (c) giving the Left the "reckoning" against former Bush administration officials that Holder promised in June 2008.

The Justice Department has spearheaded the administration's conceptual attack on the war. The phrase "war on terror" is out, deemed too redolent of Bush, too suggestive that we are not adhering to the "rule of law" (i.e., to civilian judicial protocols), and, of course, too offensive to Muslims (i.e., it implies that the Koran may actually say things like "Strike terror into God's enemies, and your enemies" – Sura 8:60). So "war" has been replaced by "overseas contingency operation" and "terror" (thanks mostly to Janet Napolitano, Obama's Homeland Security Secretary) is now "man-caused disaster." (So far "on" is still OK, but you never know.) The bellicose term "enemy combatants" has also been purged, replaced by "individuals currently detained at Guantanamo Bay." Unfortunately, that is the same formulation used to describe Cubans the Clinton administration detained when they tried to escape Castro's Workers' Paradise. To allay any confusion, Holder occasionally opts to call the combatants "individuals captured or apprehended in connection with armed conflicts and counterterrorism operations" – not quite as catchy.

Meanwhile, under the auspices of the so-called "global justice" initiative, DOJ has revived the Clinton-era framework that gave the FBI pride of place over the CIA in overseas counterterrorism cases. This entails the implicit assumption that hostile actors outside the United States are not alien enemies but criminal suspects vested with American constitutional rights. The bureau has expanded its extraterritorial role in questioning "suspects" (i.e., providing them with *Miranda* warnings that promise the assistance of free counsel during all questioning) and in the gathering of evidence. The goal is to facilitate prosecutions in the civilian justice system – with its criminal-friendly due-process standards and requirements for disclosing government intelligence.

In the first full day of his administration, President Obama promised his base that the detention center at Guantanamo Bay would be shut down within a year – a move Holder vigorously supports. But this strictly political gambit lacked any accompanying plan for dealing with those "individuals captured or apprehended in connection with armed conflicts and counterterrorism operations" – i.e., jihadists hell-bent on mass-murdering Americans, who cannot be tried in either civilian or military courts because the evidence against them is intelligence information (often gathered from foreign agencies on the condition that it not be exposed). There is an obvious legal solution to this self-imposed problem: Gitmo should remain open, consistent with the views Holder flaunted in 2002. Alas, that would prompt mutiny on the Left, for which there is no war, only war crimes – by Bush, with Gitmo near the top of the list.

So it is Holder's task to empty Gitmo gradually, while the administration quietly concedes that Obama's one-year deadline will not be met. Much to his chagrin, the attorney general has discovered that Europe's vilification of the detention camp did not mean it would be rolling out the welcome mat for the detainees. Our allies' recalcitrance prompted a Holder brainstorm: Our government should set a good example by relocating several of the detainees – i.e., terrorists trained in al Qaeda camps – *to the United States.* Dennis Blair, Obama's National Intelligence Director, even proposed that the alien terrorists receive welfare benefits from the American taxpayers they've been planning to kill, since "you can't just put them on the street." So far, Holder's flier has been shot down by Congress – both Republicans and embarrassed Democrats who were roused by a furious public. Ever sensitive to bubbling anger on the Left, the administration has also floated the possibility of moving detainees to U.S. federal prisons, or even creating what critics aptly call "Gitmo North" – an old prison in economically depressed Standish, Michigan. Unlike Gitmo, Standish is not ready to house terrorists and would thus need an infusion of stimulus money. Once thought a national security challenge, jihadism is now a shovel-ready public-works project.

Obama and Holder stress that no prisoners have escaped from federal "supermax" prisons. That, of course, is not the issue. Once the detainees are physically in the United States, the chance that federal judges will order their release here increases exponentially. Historically, moreover, incarcerated terrorists have plotted and directed attacks, urged their confederates to forge escape plots that endanger the public, and brutally assaulted prison guards in escape attempts.

Further, given the Obama DOJ's intimacy with the American Civil Liberties Union, there are other shenanigans to consider. Holder assures the public that terrorists will be securely detained in federal custody because he is empowered to order "Special Administrative Measures." SAMs are enhanced restrictions on a terrorist inmate's ability to meet with other prisoners and communicate with the outside world. Yet, while making his

> *Once thought a national security challenge, jihadism is now a shovel-ready public-works project.*

pitch, Holder didn't see fit to mention that his department was simultaneously abandoning the SAMs in the case of convicted terrorist Richard Reid, the "shoe bomber" who tried to blow up a trans-Atlantic flight with nearly 200 people aboard. As Debra Burlingame explains, after a hunger strike by Reid, the Justice Department capitulated to his risible contention that the SAMs violated the First

Amendment – including Reid's asserted right to perform daily "group prayers in a manner prescribed by my religion" (the "group" in question includes the 1993 World Trade Center bombers and other convicted terrorists). Naturally, the ACLU is using the Reid precedent to challenge the SAMs on behalf of terrorists held in other federal prisons.

Holder, meanwhile, is finding other ways to clear out Gitmo. Despite the numerous known instances of detainees returning to the battlefield, the administration has "cleared for release" scores of the 200-plus remaining prisoners. They can leave the second a country willing to take them is found – meaning that if the administration succeeds in transferring the prisoners to U.S. jails, federal judges will have a stronger basis to release them here. Just how exacting is the Justice Department's "cleared for release" standard? Well, in February, the administration sprang Binyam Mohammed. He'd been at Gitmo for six years because, in 2001, Khalid Sheikh Mohammed tried to send him to the U.S. to be the accomplice of the "dirty bomber" José Padilla in a series of mass-murder attacks targeting U.S. cities. Mohammed is now living free and clear (and on public assistance) in Britain.

And then there's the military commission system, that burr under the Leftist saddle. Its adoption was not just a thematic demonstration of seriousness about prosecuting a war as a war. As a practical matter, commission procedures lower the prosecution's bar for admitting hearsay evidence (which protects classified sources) and otherwise restrict the public disclosure of national-defense information. Although the al Qaeda Bar succeeded in persuading the Supreme Court's liberal bloc to invalidate the Bush-ordered commissions in 2006, Congress promptly authorized them later that year — underscoring the public will that jihadists not be granted the same judicial rights as the Americans they are sworn to kill. Holder and his ideologues wanted to end the system but reluctantly recognized that many combatants cannot be convicted under higher civilian court standards. So they are instead margin-

> *If anything in life remains certain, it is that America's enemies and American lawyers have no trouble finding each other.*

alizing commissions.

DOJ has worked with congressional Democrats to sculpt modifications that would force more cases into the civilian courts (e.g., removing the commissions' jurisdiction to try "material support to terrorism" offenses — a staple of terror prosecutions). Other face-saving tweaks will assure the Left that Obama commissions are not like those bad Bush commissions. Especially rich is the administration's resolve on what it claims is the difficulty enemy combatants face in retaining counsel. Granted, staffing the Obama administration has left the al Qaeda Defense Bar somewhat depleted, but if anything in life remains certain, it is that America's enemies and American lawyers have no trouble finding each other.

THE RECKONING

The most reprehensible undermining of our war footing, however, is the stunning transfer of KSM & Co. to federal court in New York.

Legally, the move makes no sense. The five jihadists were prepared to end the case by pleading guilty in the military commission a year ago. The transfer is proceeding despite the fact that the commission system is being maintained – indeed, Holder announced that the bombers of the U.S.S. Cole (who killed 17 members of the U.S. Navy) will be tried by commission, notwithstanding that a civilian indictment has been pending against them for years. By capriciously placing the worst war criminals in the civilian system, Holder gives the lesser jihadists consigned to military justice a powerful claim that they've been denied fundamental fairness. Worse, he makes a mockery of humanitarian law, which has strived for decades to civilize warfare. Wittingly or not, Holder's perverse message is: second-class justice for attacking military assets; gold-plated justice for mass-murdering civilians.

A civilian trial for KSM & Co. makes perfect sense only if it's seen as a political maneuver. The impatient Obama Left has been champing at the bit for torture and war-crimes prosecutions against government officials who formulated and carried out Bush-era counterterrorism policies, particularly interrogation. This has created a political quandary for Obama. Although the war in Iraq became unpopular, Americans strongly approve of the Bush counterterrorism measures. Hence the resonance of former Vice President Dick Cheney's withering critiques of Obama's performance. The specter of investigations against Bush officials while terrorists are coddled appeals to Obama's base but galls most Americans. The president is thus walking a fine line: vaguely telling the public he prefers "to look forward, not back," but keeping the door open for prosecutions against any Bush official "shown to have violated the law" – something that, of course, cannot be "shown" absent the investigations the administration is saying it doesn't wish to conduct . . . even as it conducts them.

Concurrently, because it is more palatable politically to publish the nation's secrets than to embrace the Third World practice of persecuting the ruling party's political adversaries, the Justice Department has pushed for disclosure of classified information. This increases the likelihood that the Left will get its reckoning from some foreign tribunal – Holder in fact told the German press in April that he was open to cooperation with European investigations of Bush "war crimes." Resuscitating the case of KSM & Co. in a civilian setting perfectly fits this template. In civilian court, defendants have an unqualified right to represent themselves – they don't have to accept a military defense lawyer with a security clearance to screen them from top-secret intelligence. It is Defense 101 that when it's obvious that the accused is guilty and that the government's investigative methods are controversial, the accused shoots for jury nullification by putting the government on trial. A civilian KSM case will be an intelligence banquet for the Left: new disclosures about coercive interrogations, "black-site" prisons, renditions, warrantless surveillance, etc. – along with the identification of witnesses who can provide sworn testimony.

The civilian case is also the next logical step in the transformation of constitutional police powers into a political cudgel. Over strenuous objections from the Defense Department and the intelligence community, Holder released memos in which the Bush Justice Department's OLC provided guidance for the CIA's enhanced interrogation program. Transparently designed to inflame the public against Bush, the move backfired – just as the KSM gambit is backfiring. The release of the memos advanced no public interest but edified our enemies about how to improve their counterinterrogation training. Nor, despite the Obamedia's obsession with torture, did Americans miss the central point of the memos: the care taken by Bush DOJ lawyers to ensure that controversial tactics (e.g., waterboarding) steered clear of the legal line of torture.

Real law enforcement, though often challenging, is straightforward: You follow the evidence wherever it leads. Politicized justice, by contrast, is complicated – populist whim mixing uneasily with legal rigor. The DOJ memo disclosure is a case in point. Obama and Holder pandered to their base by sanctimoniously pronouncing that waterboarding is torture, no matter how and why it is administered. In reality, however, Congress intentionally made torture a difficult crime to prove, requiring not only heinous inflictions of pain but proof that the interrogator had a motive to torture his victim – as opposed to, say, a motive to obtain lifesaving intelligence. So the release of the memos prompted more salivating for indictments by Obama's base while simultaneously demonstrating that there is no case.

Holder's overtly political response to this dilemma would be comical were the stakes not so high. He has ordered investigations. This enables him to tell the Left he is acting decisively while telling everyone else he hasn't done anything of consequence. So Bush administration lawyers are being probed by Justice's Office of Professional Responsibility to determine whether their guidance fell below norms of lawyerly competence. This finding could have profound professional and financial consequences for the lawyers, even though having OPR grade the scholarship of OLC is like having the Double-A batting coach critique Derek Jeter's swing. Remarkably, even as it investigates the Bush lawyers for their analysis of federal torture law, Justice has relied on that analysis in court to refute torture claims in other cases. And in astounding congressional testimony ignored by the press, Holder was forced to concede that waterboarding is not torture when government agents have a legitimate national-security purpose other than inflicting pain (e.g., training intelligence operatives to resist interrogation).

More despicably, based on a 2004 inspector-general's report, Holder reopened an investigation of six-year-old allegations against CIA interrogators – an investigation that had been closed because professional career prosecutors (i.e., not Bush political appointees) had determined that no crimes had been committed. This is as cynical as it gets: The new party in power doesn't like the objective result, so it demands a do-over. Nor is the witch hunt cost-free: The CIA officers must endure additional expense and anxiety, while the intelligence community recedes into the ethos of risk aversion that allowed 9/11 to happen.

The same political gamesmanship is at play in the administration's mishandling of classified photos depicting instances of prisoner abuse. The ACLU is endeavoring to pry them loose in a Freedom of Information Act (FOIA) lawsuit. Although no one disputes that the photos will be used by the enemy to inflame jihadis and endanger Americans, the administration wants them to be released (to appease the Left) but wants to blame disclosure on the courts as if its hands were tied (to avoid offending most Americans). Thus, Holder initially declined to appeal a disclosure order, relenting – at Obama's direction – only after outcry from the public and the military. But as this theater now moves to the Supreme Court, we should see it for the farce that it is. FOIA empowers the president to seal information whose revelation would endanger lives and harm national security. Obama could end the case today simply by issuing an executive order. He hasn't done that because of politics. And, as ever, Holder is carrying his boss's water.

That is DOJ's new leitmotif, even outside the politically charged national-security realm. The plug, for example, was recently pulled on a corruption investigation of New Mexico Governor Bill Richardson, the influential Democrat who was Obama's original choice for commerce secretary — a nomination derailed by the probe. Although the grand jury investigation was being conducted by the U.S. attorney in New Mexico, the Associated Press reported that the case was "killed in Washington" — that is, by Main Justice.

Even if you didn't know about Holder's handling of the Gore case in 1997, the Richardson whitewash should come as no surprise. In one of his first official acts as attorney general, while our ears still rang from his pious confirmation testimony about honoring DOJ processes and keeping the department above politics, Holder overruled his OLC's well-founded opinion that the controversial D.C. voting rights bill pending in Congress is unconstitutional. The bill is strongly favored by Democrats because it would give the heavily Democratic District of Columbia a representative in the House of Representatives (and lay the groundwork for eventual Senate seats as well). The infirmity, however, is blatant: The District is not a state — the Constitution plainly says House members must be chosen "by the

People of the several States." When Holder didn't like this answer from OLC, he blithely ignored DOJ protocols and turned to his friends at the Solicitor General's office (who represent the government in the Supreme Court but are not generally consulted on unenacted legislation). To them, he put a very different question – could the solicitor general defend the D.C. voting rights bill in court? – and got the desired answer. Of course, Justice is supposed to give us the *right* answer, not a wrong answer it supposes might be posited without too much embarrassment.

Embarrassment, however, abounds in the area of greatest political consequence to the Obama administration: voter fraud. As the president plummets in the polls and the Democratic Congress achieves record low approval ratings, the Justice Department has a message for those who would undermine the integrity of our elections: Have at it!

In 1993, as Democrats in Congress pushed to loosen voter-registration restrictions, Republicans insisted on a provision that required states to remove ineligible voters (people who had died or moved away) from their rolls. The Bush Justice Department used it to lodge an enforcement action against Missouri – numerous counties there sport many more registered voters than voting-age residents. Holder's Civil Division, however, has quietly dismissed the suit despite the state's noncompliance.

The department is also using the 1965 Voting Rights Act (an outdated vestige of Jim Crow) to bar states such as Georgia from using Social Security numbers and driver's license data to validate the U.S. citizenship of prospective voters, nattering that these commonsense measures have a "discriminatory effect" on minority voters. The Voting Rights Act gamesmanship achieved ludicrous heights in September. The voters of Kinston, North Carolina – a small, predominantly black town – had voted to remove party affiliations from ballots in local elections. The DOJ has told them they can't. Holder's minions "reasoned" that this could deny African-Americans their newfangled constitutional right to representation by

Democrats – or, better, deny the Democratic Party its apparent right to be elected by black voters. In sum, Justice figures that, without the right label (meaning the "D" label) next to a candidate's name, black voters cannot be trusted to decide which candidates to support.

Most astonishing, however, is the case of the New Black Panther Party. On election day 2008, Philadelphians were intimidated at polling stations by combat-clad Panthers. These Obama supporters shouted racial epithets while menacing voters, one with a nightstick. The hijinks were caught on videotape. One of the men, Jerry Jackson, was a credentialed Democratic Party poll-watcher whose MySpace page brayed about "Killing Crakkkas." The Bush Justice Department filed a civil-rights suit against three of the men. The Panthers contemptuously ignored the suit and defaulted. Yet, before damages could be assessed, Holder's Civil Rights Division withdrew the case after the government had already won. The case was ultimately dismissed outright against two of the defendants.

As to the third – the nightstick-wielding Samir Shabazz – DOJ fecklessly agreed to an injunction prohibiting him from displaying a weapon at a polling place for the next three years. (That's like settling a bank-robbery case by getting the robber to agree not to rob any more banks for three years). The U.S. Civil Rights Commission is demanding disclosure of DOJ's deliberations and rationale for abandoning the case. Despite his promise of a new era of transparency, Holder is doing what Holder does: He is stonewalling, just as he ignored the efforts of congressional Republicans to obtain the same information. It's not a complete stalemate, though. Thanks to the dismissal, Jerry Jackson has gotten his poll-watcher credentials back. Next election season, he'll be right back in business.

By then, while CIA agents and Bush officials mortgage their homes to pay legal fees, KSM will be settled in New York, with a team of lawyers combing through American intelligence files to prepare for his trial. That's politics . . . but it's not justice.

First American edition published in 2010 by Encounter Books,
an activity of Encounter for Culture and Education, Inc.,
a nonprofit, tax exempt corporation.
Encounter Books website address: www.encounterbooks.com

Manufactured in the United States and printed on
acid-free paper. The paper used in this publication meets
the minimum requirements of ANSI/NISO 39.48–1992
(R 1997) (*Permanence of Paper*).

LIBRARY OF CONGRESS CATALOGING-IN-PUBLICATION DATA

McCarthy, Andrew C.
How the Obama administration has politicized justice /
by Andrew C. McCarthy.
p. cm. — (Encounter broadsides)
ISBN-13: 978-1-59403-474-9 (pbk. : alk. paper)
ISBN-10: 1-59403-474-5 (pbk. : alk. paper)
1. Law enforcement—Political aspects—United States.
2. Justice, Administration of—Political aspects—United States.
3. United States. Dept. of Justice. I. Title.
HV8139.M33 2009
364.973—dc22
2009043919

10 9 8 7 6 5 4 3 2 1